T0368594

There's P-nut Butter in this BOOK!

D.K. Robertson

WestBow Press books may be ordered through booksellers or by contacting:

WestBow Press
A Division of Thomas Nelson & Zondervan
1663 Liberty Drive
Bloomington, IN 47403
www.westbowpress.com
844-714-3454

ISBN: 979-8-3850-3438-3 (sc)
ISBN: 979-8-3850-3439-0 (e)

Library of Congress Control Number: 2024920176

Print information available on the last page.

WestBow Press rev. date: 12/05/2024

WestBow
PRESS®
A DIVISION OF THOMAS NELSON
& ZONDERVAN

THIS BOOK has little Smudges

of BROWN and

STICKY RED

There's Pages that
Won't TURN
AND **WORDS**

AXZTIN

STK.

Zytte

that can't be
SAID!

It Looks Like

fUNNY

Finger Prints

and PIECES OF

OLD
TOAST

It Has Some Odd
WEiRD Smells

But of PEANUTS
it smells
the MOST!

Now <u>WHO</u> A

READS

PICTURE

BOOK

WHILE EATING <u>ALL</u>

THIS STUFF

?

Bananas,

MUSTARD,

PICKLE
JUICE

Some Pages
are ALL
DOG
EARED

I Think
THEY'RE
ALL
STUCK
with
GUM!

GUM

mmmm...... Smells like DOUBLE BUBBLE.

Believe I'd sure like Some!

How can We
go on

and READ this

NASTY

BOOK

?

the PUPPY has EATEN PAGES

and
some

HE EVEN

TOOK
!

SO . . . . . .
We'll Just
Pick ANOTHER

to READ
That'd Be
my
MOOD

THE
BOOK
OF
PIZZA

BUT

SOAP

WASH

Your FACE

and

HANDS

our BOOKS can't look Like FOOD!

Now like this
Damaged
BOOK,
We ALL are
Just as
STAINED

We may lie or Cheat or HATE or ignore THEIR needs

NOT DO GOOD as we were TRAINED

But GOD forgives and TEACHES us To FOLLOW GREATER WAYS →

THIS = BOOK should GUIDE Our DAYS

HOLY BIBLE

JANUARY APRIL MAY
FEBRUARY JUNE JULY
AUGUST
MARCH OCTOBER
SEPTEMBR

NOVEMBR
DECEMBER

SUNDAY	MONDAY	TUESDAY	WEDNESDAY	THURSDAY	FRIDAY	SATURDAY

PSALMS 24:3,4

Printed in the United States
by Baker & Taylor Publisher Services